Bible Explorers

Welcome to the World of

Wizzy Gizmo™

Dear Reader,

The Wizzy Gizmo series is more than fun-filled stories. It is an in-depth exposition of the Bible, book-by-book. Yes, it is filled with fun stories, but never will we compromise on accurately following the text of God's Word. Why? Because we believe:

"All Scripture is inspired by God and profitable for teaching, for reproof, for correction, for training in righteousness, that the man of God may be adequate, equipped for every good work."

II Timothy 3:16,17

Old Testament Series - Book One

Who Created Everything?

Chris Del Aguila & Justin Cummins

General Editor: Dr. David Beverly

Ilustrated by: Justin Cummins

EOG Studios, Publisher

This is a work of fiction and non-fiction. The Wizzy Gizmo characters, places, and incidents are either products of the authors imagination or, if real are used fictitiously.

Chris Del Aguila and Justin Cummins
Cover by: Justin Cummins
General Editor: Dr. David Beverly
Editor: Janea Beakley
Illustrations by: Justin Cummins, Grace Cummins and Victoria Cummins

Library of Congress Catalog-in-Publication Data
EOG Studios, 2013 Wizzy Gizmo Old Testament Series Book One:
Who Created Everything?

Summary: The kids of Sunnyville experience an incredible adventure as they explore the wonders of Creation.

ISBN-10: 0-9898245-0-0
ISBN-13: 978-0-9898245-0-7

Printed in the U.S.A.

Additional resources available at www.wizzygizmo.com

CONTENTS

Wizzy Gizmo is a world famous inventor and Professor of Science & Technology at Sunnyville University. Possibly his most significant invention is Gizmovision, a device which brings any book to life with the touch of a button.

Qwacky is robot duck that can't quite seem to figure out how to be a proper duck. He thinks he is a dog, or a tiger, or a lion, or maybe a parrot, or even an eagle. This problem is compounded by the fact that he can transform in to anything he wants.

Pepe, whose full name is actually Praxedis López Ramos, is Wizzy Gizmo's pet dog. He has an advantage over other dogs, because he can think and speak through an invention Wizzy likes to call, *the Anama-Gizmo-Logic.*

Summer is the oldest, most reserved and mature of the Sunnyville kids. Age 9, she's always concerned about everyone's safety and wellbeing. She loves to read and is always ready to share from her wealth of knowledge.

Thomas is outgoing and fun. He loves to do adventurous things and is bursting with energy. He tends to find himself in extraordinary situations. He loves to play guitar and ride his skateboard. He is 7.

Eli is shy, but very observant. He loves history and science and wants to be a pilot or astronaut one day. He has a fascination for rockets and builds them as a hobby. He is 8.

Olive never walks, she runs, and barefoot at that. Age 7, she loves animals and is always chasing them, trying to hold them and pet them. She loves the outdoors, rivers, parks, mountains, etc.

Gizmovision

THE LONG AWAITED SUMMER had finally come. Every kid in Sunnyville was bursting with excitement. You see, the last day of school was over and done with, finished, and kaput! All down the streets of the town kids were running, skipping, and generally glorying in newfound freedom. Down by the river, kids were frolicking and swimming. At the park kids were twirling and skipping rope. In the trees above the green grass they were climbing while singing. Every kid in town was out playing, all except one. Eli was new in town, and he hadn't made any friends yet. So Eli was not running, or swimming, or climbing, or spinning, or frolicking. He wasn't jumping, or dancing, or playing, or singing. No, Eli was all alone.

On this scorching hot Saturday afternoon, Eli found himself sitting under the biggest and oldest tree in Giant Oak Park. He sat with his back propped up against the tree slowly licking on a red and blue snow cone. Beams of sunlight danced all around him as the breeze rustled the leaves above. Robins fluttered from tree to tree, chirping at each other. In the clearing, two squirrels chased each other back and forth, playing the ancient game of squirrel tag. He watched as a group of yelling boys came bounding out of a thicket, chasing a terrified rabbit down the path, up a grassy hill and into the forest.

"I sure wish I had somebody to play with," he sighed as he took another lick of his snow cone. That's when it happened.

Boing! Something bounced off his head.

"Ouch! Who threw that?"

Eli looked around a bit dazed and confused. Looking up, Eli was surprised to find a little redheaded girl staring back at him with a sheepish grin. There was a playful air about her. Her emerald-green eyes twinkled *gaily* with silent laughter. He knew immediately she would be a good friend.

"Hello," she called down. "Please forgive me, I didn't see you down there!"

"That's okay," Eli kindly responded. "My mom says I have a hard head. Or maybe she meant to say that I'm hardheaded," Eli added, while still rubbing the *throbbing* bump on his head. The little girl laughed and asked,

"What's your name?"

Eli responded, "My mom and dad call me Elijah, but my friends call me Eli. What about you?"

"Well," said the girl thoughtfully, "if I'm in BIG trouble, my mom calls me Olivia Cora Sanderson, but all my friends call me Olive."

"Olive," Eli echoed, repeating her name. He had learned this from his grandfather, who always told him that repeating someone's name out loud helps you remember it.

"My family and I just moved here from the big city," replied Eli.

Olive had never, in her short life, been to the big city, and she was very curious about it. Her mind whirled with all sorts of questions for Eli. For instance, how did those towering skyscrapers stay up without falling? Or why do trains travel under the city? And what kinds of animals live in a concrete jungle? Just as Olive was going to ask Eli another question, they were interrupted by the arrival of two of Olive's friends. One was a slightly older black-haired girl riding a red beachcomber bike. The other was a younger boy who was wearing a blue letterman jacket, zipping back and forth on his red skateboard.

"Hi Summer, hi Thomas, what's going on?" called out Olive.

"Olive, Olive... he's finished! Wizzy finished it!" blurted out Thomas, whipping the skateboard to a stop.

"Finished what?" asked Olive.

"I think what Thomas is trying to say is that Wizzy finally finished his new invention. He's waiting for us at his workshop," explained Summer.

Now, I can hear you asking yourself, "Who is Wizzy?" Well, Wizzy is short for Professor Wizzy Gizmo. He is a superfabulicious, *hyper-inteligent* inventor who loves to invent all sorts of *gadgets* and *gizmos*. Inventions like toasters that can dance, or one-size-fits-all pants, spoons that like to fence, and even robot ants that water plants. Everyone in town loved Wizzy, and Eli was about to discover why.

"Who's Wizzy?" asked Eli.

"Well new kid, we could tell you who Wizzy is, but I think it's better if you see him with your own eyes," replied Thomas. "Come on, follow me! I'll show you the way."

A few minutes later, on the other side of town, Eli got his first look at the Gizmo Shack. It sat atop a small hill right next to a small orchard of apple trees. On the other side there was an overgrown vegetable garden, which was currently being devoured by a family of pigs, snorting merrily. The shack itself was an odd sort of building, not square like most. It was wider at the top and had strange smoke stacks sticking out all over the roof. The windows were all different shapes and scattered all over the shop. Eli was filled with anticipation and wonder as he thought about what could possibly be inside.

Thomas walked boldly up to the door and knocked. There was no answer. Summer walked up and together, she and Thomas knocked, rapped, and banged on the door.

They heard the muffled sound of beeping computers and gadgets clicking and ticking, but still no answer. Finally, Olive and Eli joined them, and together they all knocked, bopped, slapped, rapped, banged, clanged, and even rang the doorbell.

Now, they heard all sorts of bangs, boings, bonks, clanks, clatters, and crashes.

"Ahhh!" a voice inside yelled. "Wait Qwacky, not the goat milk!"

There was one final crash of breaking glass.

"Well... better see who's at the door," a voice deep inside the shack sighed.

As the door **creaked** open Eli got his first look at Wizzy. Wow! Wizzy was a sight to see—messy bluish hair and **knobby** knees. He had a pencil **perched** behind his ear, and behind his square black rimmed glasses his eyes sparkled with cheer. Inside the house all sorts of gadgets lay here and there, some so odd you just had to stare. There were tiny robot ants marching towards a planter in the back. To their left, two spoons were engaged in a lively duel, fighting furiously on a windowsill. By the coffee machine, a toaster was dancing to the tune of an Irish jig. In the middle of the shop was a robot duck that was stuck under a heap of stuff. He had big eyes, tank treads for feet, a silly hat, and wore a goofy smile on his robot beak. On the other side of the room sat a normal looking dog, in a normal looking chair, reading a normal looking cookbook.

"Hi, Wizzy!" called out the children.

"Hey everybody," Wizzy smiled back.

Eli stood in the doorway, with his mouth open. He didn't know what was stranger, the bluish hair, the robot duck, or a dog that could read, not to mention all the other strange looking gizmos dancing and moving all over the place.

"Who might you be?" Wizzy asked noticing Eli for the first time.

"My name is Eli," replied the shy brown-headed boy.

"I see," Wizzy responded. "Well, young sir, you picked a most *auspicious* day to come to my workshop."

"What does auspicious mean?" asked Eli.

Suddenly, the robot duck sprang up into the air sending gadgets and tools flying everywhere. Music began blasting from somewhere inside his body and he sang out:

**"Auspicious must be real delicious,
Makes me think it's quite nutritious,
Gonna keep me healthy inside,
Slice it, dice it, give it to me fried."**

The normal looking dog, that had been quietly reading, looked up and asked in a rich, Spanish accent, "Qwacky, what exactly do you think auspicious means?"

"Eeeeeasy!" sang out Qwacky, with a tone of *unmitigated* confidence in his voice, "auspicious is a tasty snack."

"My dear duck," Pepe chuckled, "auspicious means

well-timed."

Wizzy, looking quite amused continued, "Now here's why it's an auspicious day to visit my workshop." He walked over to a table on the other side of the shop and pulled the cover off. A small glass box covered with circuits, buttons, and flashing lights lay on the table.

"What is it?" all the kids asked in excitement.

"It's GIZMOVISION!" Wizzy declared.

"What does it do?" Olive wondered aloud.

"To put it simply," answered Wizzy, "it *transforms* any book into a life-like world inside a virtual bubble! You don't just see the story—you touch it, taste it, feel it, and even smell it, all inside this bubble!"

"Would you kids like to try it out?"

The kids were so excited they could hardly contain themselves.

Wizzy rubbed his chin, thinking aloud, "What book should we begin with?"

Thomas ran over to the bookshelves, pulled out a book titled, *Blazing Trails Through the Wild West,* and asked, "What about this book about cowboys?" Qwacky's hat suddenly transformed into a ten-gallon cowboy hat as Qwacky *pranced* around the room challenging the spoons to a duel.

Olive looked intently at the books and asked, "What about a story about a princess who lives in a beautiful

castle?" Qwacky's cowboy hat changed into a lovely pink princess hat. The dueling spoons stopped fighting and started giggling at him. Summer found a dusty old book with a picture of a pyramid on the front. "*Mumford's Mother Lode of Mummies*" she read out loud. "Or maybe not," she decided.

"Hey, what about this?" Eli asked excitedly, holding a book named *Dinosaur Explorers.* Qwacky jumped up on a bench and roared so loudly the robot ants squeaked, and fell off the plant they were watering.

Wizzy walked over to his desk and *fumbled* around until he found a well-worn book. "Why not a book that will take us all the way back to the very beginning, before cowboys, princesses, Egyptians, or even dinosaurs?"

Wondering what old and mysterious book Wizzy had picked, Eli asked, "Wizzy, which book is that?"

"This book contains the words of the Creator, the One who made the universe and everything in it. It's called the Bible!"

"Wow!" the kids said in awe, "that sounds amazing!"

Wizzy carefully set the Bible in the center of his Gizmovision invention and flicked a button. The machine whirled and hummed, the room began to vibrate and shake, and the lights started to flicker on and off. The invention was surrounded by tiny arcs of electricity, as a sphere of blue-green light emerged and began to grow bigger and bigger. There was a flash, and then...

CHAPTER 2

Day One of Creation

DARKNESS. A COLD, SILENT, empty darkness seemed to stretch on forever and ever. The kids were scared.

"Wizzy, what happened?" cracked Summer's voice as she whispered, "I can't see a thing."

Olive asked fearfully, "Where is everything? It's so dark!"

"I'm scared," squeaked Thomas.

"No need to worry there, Thomas," Wizzy reassured him, "my invention is working just fine. You see, before God created everything, there was nothing."

"Nothing," the kids echoed in wonder.

"Absolutely," answered Wizzy. "God made everything out of nothing. Theologians call that *ex nihilo* which is Latin for 'out of nothing.' The Bible will show us how He did it."

Without warning, a deep resounding voice thundered into the darkness around them.

"In the beginning God created the heavens and the earth."
Genesis 1:1

"Wait a second, you're saying that God made *EVERYTHING?*" questioned Eli.

"Not me, the Word of God tells us this," responded Wizzy. "That booming voice you just heard coming from my invention is speaking the word of God, the Bible. And the Bible tells us God is *infinitely* powerful. In fact, He made the whole universe, the planets, the stars—everything!"

"Hyperquakofackotantistic!" quacked Qwacky.

"What did He make it from Wizzy?" Summer questioned.

"It's quite astounding that God made everything out of nothing. All God did was speak and the world was created, simply by the power of His word!"

At that very moment, the thunderous voice returned echoing in the pitch-black darkness.

"The earth was formless and void, and darkness was over the surface of the deep, and the Spirit of God was moving over the surface of the waters."

Genesis 1:2

"Wait a second, I still can't see the earth!" Thomas said, concerned as he peered intently into the surrounding darkness.

"Hmm, let's see. What are we missing? Why can't we see it?" Wizzy wondered.

"Then God said, 'Let there be light': and there was light. God saw that the light was good; and God separated the light from the darkness."

Genesis 1:3,4

The whole universe seemed to explode in a symphony of light. The light reached out, pushing away the darkness forcing everyone to cover their eyes with their hands or paws.

"Whoa!" Qwacky said. "Somebody get my sunglasses for me!"

"Look!" said Thomas in wonder. "I can see the earth now!"

"I don't know if I like being this high above the earth," said Eli nervously as he grabbed onto Pepe's tail.

"It's beautiful!" Olive whispered in awe as she gazed down at the shimmering blue planet.

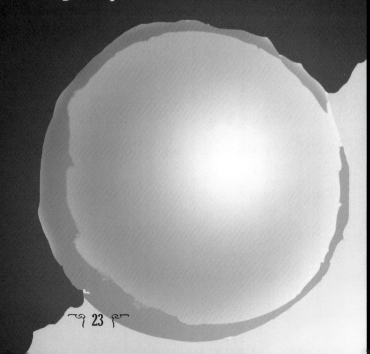

"I'm glad God made light. The dark is too scary!" Thomas said with relief in his voice.

"God made the light and dark so we could have day and night," Wizzy explained.

"God called the light day, and the darkness He called night. And there was evening and there was morning, one day."
Genesis 1:5

"This is incredible! I can't believe this is the very first day ever," marveled Summer.

The light began to fade all around them as they orbited around to the night side of the earth. Thomas floated over to Wizzy and asked, "Why is it getting dark again? I didn't even see the sun set."

"You're right Thomas; I never even saw the sun!" Eli exclaimed.

"And where are the moon and the stars?" followed Thomas as he eyed the empty night sky.

"Excellent questions," Wizzy answered. "On the first day of creation, God made the earth and light. He had not made the sun, the moon, or the stars yet. Remember, there are still five days of creation left."

"Wait, there's more?" Eli asked in astonishment.

"You better believe it," said Pepe.

"Are you ready for day two?" Wizzy laughed. The kids could hardly wait.

Day Two of Creation

"Then God said, 'Let there be an expanse
[or *firmament*] in the midst of the waters, and let it
separate the waters from the waters.'"

Genesis 1:6

"Firma-what?" asked Qwacky.

"*Firmament*, mi amigo, is simply a fancy word for
space," Pepe answered.

"Exactly, Pepe," Wizzy said, "you see how the earth
is covered by water? Well, God is about to take some of
that water and expand it into space!"

"You mean God is going to take all the waters off
the earth?" Eli asked.

"No. Look!" Summer watched. "He's leaving some."

**"God made the expanse, and separated the
waters which were below the expanse from the
waters which were above the expanse: and it was
so."**

Genesis 1:7

"Here comes the rest…watch out!" Thomas shouted
as the water rose up and expanded out like a giant balloon

around the earth. It kept getting bigger and bigger as it reached out in every direction into space. The water roared past them in a giant expanding wave instantly soaking them from head to foot.

"I love water fights," Olive giggled.

"Oh no, no one likes the wet dog smell," moaned Pepe.

"Jumping jalapeños!" Qwacky quacked. "It's time for some hot air."

Eli watched in wonder as Qwacky's arms folded in, and his tank treads seemed to melt away. Within seconds, Qwacky had transformed himself into a giant blow dryer. The kids felt like they were caught in a scorching tornado as their hair was blown in every direction, and their shirts and pants flapped all over the place.

Again, the immense voice rang out saying:

"God called the expanse heaven. And there was evening and there was morning, a second day."
Genesis 1:8

"You mean heaven where God is?" Thomas asked.

"Well, in this case, the word heaven is talking about the space above the earth," Wizzy explained.

"You mean God just made space?"

"Super galactic!" Qwacky exclaimed.

"It's really c-c-o-l-l-d-d in space," Olive shivered.

"Right, what am I thinking?" Wizzy said. "After all, this is Gizmovision, where you not only see, but hear, touch, smell, and feel everything. Let's see what we can do."

Wizzy began pressing buttons on a device he wore on his wrist. The kids heard beeping and blipping, pinging and ringing. Wizzy was up to something. When he had finished pressing all those buttons, he pressed a large red button on the end of the device. Without warning, a large red car appeared out of nowhere. It had rocket boosters and wings on the sides.

"I call it the Gizmoblaster and it can transform into any kind of vehicle we need it to be," declared Wizzy. The Gizmoblaster sputtered awake as the powerful engine *chortled* and *throttled* and finally roared to life.

"Wow! Does it go crazy fast?" Thomas asked *eagerly*.

"Oh goodness, I'm sure it'll go fast enough Thomas." Summer laughed.

"Okay everyone hop in," Wizzy encouraged them.

The kids jumped into the Gizmoblaster, scrambled into the back seats, and strapped on their seatbelts. Wizzy jumped into the driver's seat with Pepe and Qwacky in tow.

"Pedal to the metal," *quipped* Qwacky.

"...And there was evening and there was morning, a second day."
Genesis 1:8b

"I wonder what day three has in store for us?" asked
Wizzy with a knowing grin.

Day Three of Creation

"Then God said, 'Let the waters below the heavens be gathered into one place, and let the dry land appear'; and it was so."

Genesis 1:9

"Wow!" The kids were amazed.

"Let's zoom in for a closer look!" Wizzy suggested as he revved the powerful engines. Faster than the kids could reply, the Gizmoblaster accelerated forward and went zipping down towards the surface of the earth.

"Woohoo!" Thomas shouted "Faster, Faster!"

"Hang on!" Wizzy hit the *accelerator*, pushing them all back in their seats. The Gizmoblaster swooped down and *skimmed* the surface of the great ocean. Pepe's tongue was flapping up and down, and his cheeks ballooned out as he hung his head out of the window. Wizzy took the wheel and spun it hard, sending the Gizmoblaster into a whirling spin.

"Wizzy, you're making us dizzy!" cried the kids.

"Galloping gophers, I think I'm going to be sick," *groaned* Qwacky.

Wizzy slowed down so they could see the dry land

appear.

"Hey look, everybody," Eli said as he pointed, "the land is rising." The water roared as it gathered into one place. The land was creaking and groaning as it rose above the water.

"We have somewhere to stand now," Eli said in relief.

"Oh good, now we can have a picnic too!" Olive said with excitement.

"God called the dry land earth, and the gathering of the waters He called seas; and God saw that it was good." Genesis 1:10

"Time to land the Gizmoblaster on the earth," Wizzy told them. The Gizmoblaster landed quietly and softly. The kids unfastened their seatbelts and the door opened with a loud *hiss.*

"Do you want to explore?" Wizzy asked them knowing the answer.

"Yes!" all the kids shouted. They stepped out of the Gizmoblaster and the ground crunched under their feet. Looking around, they were met by the sight of vacant and empty land. A low-pitched *drone* filled the air—the wind howled.

"Hey, where's the grass?" Eli asked.

"Or trees to climb?" Olive added.

"Or flowers to pick?" Summer said as she looked

around desperately.

"The land looks so lonely," Olive said sadly.

"Don't worry. God is still not done. Wait and see what God does next!" Wizzy said.

"Then God said, 'Let the earth sprout vegetation; plants yielding seed, *and* fruit trees on the earth bearing fruit after their kind with seed in them', and it was so. The earth brought forth vegetation, plants yielding seed after their kind, and trees bearing fruit with seed in them, after their kind; and God saw that it was good."

Genesis 1:11,12

Suddenly, the lonely land began to change. No longer was it desolate and bare. A world of plants sprouted and grew all around them. The world was coming to life.

"Oh look! The grass is growing right beneath our feet," giggled Summer as the growing grass tickled her feet.

"And look at all the trees, they're all so beautiful!" Olive cried as trees of all shapes and sizes filled the land.

Qwacky was rolling back and forth on the grass, and Pepe was scratching his back on the nearest tree. Wizzy and kids set off to explore this amazing assortment of plants that went as far as the eye could see. They walked through grass that was as tall as a full-grown horse and passed trees that rose up high above. The smell of spring was in the air; everything smelled new and fresh.

"Hey look, sunflowers!" cried out Eli.

"Why don't you pick some seeds and do a taste test?" Wizzy suggested.

"Sunflower seeds, my favorite!" Thomas exclaimed hungrily. The kids crunched and munched the seeds. Summer looked ahead to a grove of familiar looking trees.

"Hey! I found the other kind of plant! You know the kind that bears fruit!" said Summer excitedly.

"Fruit plants!" yelled all the kids.

"Apple trees!" noticed Summer as she plucked a big, juicy, red apple from the tree she was standing under.

"Look, strawberries!" Olive pointed towards a bunch of strawberry bushes and then proceeded to collect as many strawberries as would fit in her hand.

"Mangos!" Thomas cried with *fervor* as he scrambled up the mango tree and started throwing mangos down to Pepe and Qwacky. The kids chomped and chewed, crunched and munched, and got so full they felt like they were going to explode.

"Wow, now that was tasty," Wizzy patted his tummy.

"Does anyone know what else God designed plants to do?"

"They make oxygen. It's what we breathe!" Eli said thoughtfully.

"That's right, Eli. We couldn't survive without

oxygen," Wizzy explained to them.

"They also make everything look so pretty," Olive said with a *sigh*.

"They certainly make our world beautiful," Wizzy agreed. "You could say all these things reflect the power and wisdom of God."

The tallest trees began to cast long shadows as the evening neared.

"It's getting dark again Wizzy," Eli observed.

"And, there are still no stars in the night sky," said Thomas.

"If you ask me, it's kind of hair-raising," said Pepe.

There was evening and there was morning, a third day.
Genesis 1:13

"Well let's fast forward and see what happens on the fourth day of Creation!" Wizzy pressed a button on his wrist controller and suddenly, everything around them seemed to speed up until they saw the sky begin to

glow with the light of morning.

"What's that over there?" Olive asked.

CHAPTER 5

Day Four of Creation

"THE SKY IS TURNING a lighter blue," Eli exclaimed.

"Wait, something's rising in the sky!" Summer told the group.

"The sun!" Thomas cried out in delight as he pointed towards the brilliant glow of the very first sunrise.

"Suntastic!" joked Qwacky as everyone laughed.

"Then God said, 'Let there be lights in the expanse of the heavens to separate the day from the night, and let them be for signs and for seasons and for days and years; and let them be for lights in the expanse of the heavens to give light on the earth'; and it was so." **Genesis 1:14,15**

"You see," Wizzy explained, "God made the sun, moon, and stars so we could keep track of time, day from night, months, years, and seasons."

"You mean like winter, spring, summer, and fall?" Eli asked.

"Exactly!" Wizzy said excitedly.

"I see, so that's how trees know when to grow fruit," Olive said.

"Like mangos," Thomas said rubbing his belly.

"Or when to drop their leaves," Summer added.

"Oh! Jumping in a great big pile of leaves is so much fun," said Olive with a smile.

"God made the two great lights, the greater light to govern the day, and the lesser light to govern the night; He made the stars also... and God saw that it was good." Genesis 1:16, 18b

"Is the greater light the sun?" asked Summer.

"And is the lesser light the moon?" asked Eli.

"Absolutely!" replied Wizzy.

"I still can't see the stars," Olive said confused, as she stared into the blue sky.

"When the sun is up, it's hard to see any of the stars. How about we fly up there and take a closer look?" asked Wizzy.

"Into space?" Thomas exclaimed in amazement.

The kids could not believe it. To fly far above the earth, up, up into the sky and see the universe with their very own eyes, was something they had never dreamed they would do.

"Everyone back into the Gizmoblaster," Wizzy

yelled. The kids ran back to the car and piled in quickly.

"Everyone ready?" Wizzy asked as the kids strapped themselves in.

"Gizmoblast!" all the kids yelled.

The engine roared to life pressing the kids back into their seats. They rose quickly above the clouds, and then Wizzy pressed the big red button. The afterburner kicked in with a hard thump, sending them rocketing into space.

"Whoa!" the kids screamed.

"Pick up the pace, we're going into space!" Qwacky quacked. Straight up they soared into the air, past the clouds, and past the sky. So fast, that before Qwacky could say, "banana cheese pickles," they found themselves flying in space.

"Look at all those stars! They're so beautiful and sparkly," Olive said in wonder.

"Indeed they are!" Wizzy agreed. "Anyone know how many there are?"

"Let me see. One, two, three, four, five, six...," Qwacky counted faster and faster until his circuits started smoking.

"Careful, amigo!" Pepe called out to Qwacky. "There are hundreds of billions of galaxies, and each one has billions and billions of stars."

"Wow!" The kids were stunned.

"And that's only counting the ones we can see!" Wizzy said. They sat there for a long time, *gazing* at the stars, pointing out galaxies and constellations, and marveling at the majesty and power of God, the Creator. They had just found Alpha-Centauri, which happens to be the closest star to earth, when Thomas noticed he was sweating.

"Hey, Wizzy, why is it getting so hot?" Thomas asked.

"That's because we're zooming right past the sun," Wizzy cried out as he banked the Gizmoblaster into a tight turn. They narrowly missed flying right into the sun as Wizzy corkscrewed the craft into a gut wrenching turn.

"Ahhhhh!" The kids yelled as the Gizmoblaster rocketed around the sun, barely making it past a solar flare that had just erupted.

"Muy caliente!" exclaimed Pepe.

"'Too hot' is right Pepe! One more minute and I'd be roast duck!" joked Qwacky. They zoomed away from the sun and began their return trip to the earth, amazed at the glory of the heavens that God had created.

"I wonder what God will do next?" pondered Wizzy aloud as he thought about how the beauty of the heavens reminded him of Psalm 19:1-2.

**"The heavens are telling of the glory of God;
And their expanse is declaring the work of His hands.
Day to day pours forth speech,
And night to night reveals knowledge."**

Psalm 19:1,2

Day Five of Creation

THEY ENTERED THE EARTH'S atmosphere so fast they were streaking across the sky like a meteor. Wizzy held on with all his might as the Gizmoblaster was shaking uncontrollably. The lower they went, the thicker the air became. Suddenly without warning, the air exploded with a sonic boom, which shook the craft violently. They swooped down past the clouds and turned up sharply as Wizzy expertly handled the controls. The Gizmoblaster stopped shaking as they slowed down, and they found themselves cruising over the surface of the great ocean.

"Then God said, 'Let the waters teem with swarms of living creatures...'"
Genesis 1:20a

"Look down below," Olive put her hand over her mouth. She couldn't believe it. She had never been to the ocean, and had never played in the sand at the beach, or felt the crashing of the waves, or even seen any of the sea creatures she'd often read about, like whales, sharks, seals or...

"Dolphins!" Summer screeched. "Please can we go lower?"

"Sure thing!" Wizzy said.

Wizzy lowered the windows and the cool salty ocean air rushed in. The dolphins leapt in and out of the water, as the whole pod whistled and clicked, as if saying, "Hello," to the children.

"Hello, dolphins!" called out Olive, secretly wishing she could convince one to let her hop on for a ride.

"It sure would be super cool to see what's underwater!" Eli imagined out loud.

"No problem!" Wizzy said. "Activating Giz-formation!" The vehicle began to shake and shudder. The wheels tucked in and the car got impossibly longer. The rear bumper twisted and folded into a propeller. Piece by piece, part by part, the vehicle became something else as it fell from the sky and plunged straight down into the water.

"Ahhh!" yelled the kids as they splashed into the water.

"No need to worry kids," Wizzy reassured them. "The Gizmoblaster just transformed into a submarine, or as I like to call it, a Giz-marine."

It was simply amazing. They stared out into the deep blue ocean, as thousands of shapes swam in different directions all around them. There were schools of small fish that seemed to dance as they reflected sunlight off their glistening scales. There were larger shapes in the deep that cruised along, unconcerned with what happened in the shallower waters.

"Wow! Look out there!" Thomas said. "I see hundreds of jellyfish!"

"Look down there," Eli pointed, "starfish."

"Where did the dolphins go?" Olive asked *wistfully*.

Just a moment later, a loud *proximity* alarm went off. The kid's covered their ears as a siren blared and a harsh red light flashed on and off.

"What's wrong?" asked Summer fearfully.

Long slithery tentacles began wrapping themselves around the Gizmoblaster. They were covered with hundreds of suction cups that clung to the windows.

"It's a giant octopus!" Eli screamed.

"AHHHHHHH!"

The alarm continued screeching as the kid's shrieked in terror. The lights flashed on and off, and then suddenly, the tentacles were gone.

"What happened?" Summer asked. "I thought the octopus was going to reach in and have one of us for breakfast."

"You have to remember Summer, that when God first made the earth and the creatures, there still wasn't any sin. So there couldn't be any death. This Octopus probably just wanted to tickle us" Wizzy joked as the children laughed. Thomas *peered* out of the window and caught a peek of a *massive* creature swimming by.

"It's HUGE, what is it?" Thomas asked.

"I think it might be a giant Leviathan—a kind of

giant sea creature God made at the beginning," Wizzy explained.

"Let's see what else God made on the fifth day of creation. Everyone prepare for Giz-formation. Let's head back up to the sky!"

Wizzy turned the craft up towards the surface of the water and hit the pedal. Everyone was pushed back into their seats as the Gizmoblaster screamed through the water gaining speed. The craft broke through the surface of the water, much like a humpback whale might, and continued climbing into the sky as it transformed once again into a flying machine.

"Then God said... 'and let birds fly above the earth in the open expanse of the heavens.'"
Genesis 1:20

Up and up they flew high into the sky, until they got lost inside some thick cumulus clouds. As they broke through into the open sky, they found themselves flying alongside whole flocks of flying creatures.

"This is incredible; we're flying with the eagles!" Eli cried out in amazement.

"And look down there," Summer said, "I think those are ***pterodactyls***."

"And ducks," Eli said as he pointed towards a flock of ducks flying west. One of the ducks seemed confused as it kept bumping into the duck flying next to it.

"Hey, wait a second, that duck looks kind of funny,"

Thomas pointed out.

"Qwacky!" The kids laughed as one of the larger and angrier ducks chased Qwacky off.

"How did you get out there?" Wizzy shouted down to him.

"Qwack-a-doodle-dooooo!" quacked Qwacky as he flew up right next to the Gizmoblaster.

The kids were rolling in their seats laughing.

"I think you scared all the ducks away, Qwacky!" quipped Thomas.

"Aww, qwackers!" Qwacky said.

"God created the great sea monsters and every living creature that moves, with which the waters swarmed after their kind, and every winged bird after its kind; and God saw that it was good."
Genesis 1:21

"God sure made a lot of different kinds of flying animals and sea creatures," Summer said.

"It reveals how intelligent and creative God is, as we observe the *complexity* and *diversity* of creation!" Wizzy added.

"God blessed them, saying, 'Be fruitful and multiply, and fill the waters in the seas, and let birds multiply on the earth.'"
Genesis 1:22

"What does that mean?" Thomas asked.

"It means that God gave the birds and fish the ability to have babies," Wizzy said. "Does anyone know how fish and birds are born?"

"They hatch from eggs!" Eli answered.

"That's right Eli!" Wizzy said.

"Yum, scrambled eggs," Thomas sighed as he rubbed his belly.

"You better not be touching any duck eggs," Qwacky quacked, creating another *uproar* of laughter from the children.

The loud voice boomed,

"There was evening and there was morning, a fifth day."
                                                    Genesis 1:23

"Wow! What an amazing fifth day," Wizzy said. "Are you ready for more?"

"Yeah!" All the kids shouted.

Day Six of Creation

"Then God said, 'Let the earth bring forth living creatures after their kind: cattle and creeping things and beasts of the earth after their kind'; and it was so. God made the beasts of the earth after their kind, and the cattle after their kind, and everything that creeps on the ground after its kind; and God saw that it was good."

Genesis 1:24,25

Olive looked down below and saw giant and enormous creatures moving accross the land. They plowed through the forest, shoving past the trees.

"What are those?" Olive asked in astonishment.

"I think they're dinosaurs!" Summer cried out. "They're so big. Do you think I could ride one?"

"Let's fly down and take a look," Wizzy said.

Wizzy pushed the controls forward, flying the craft down toward the forest where the girls had seen the dinosaurs. The Gizmoblaster swooped down swiftly and gently into a small clearing. The children got out of the vehicle in a hurry and raced over to a small hill. As they stood there watching, they felt the ground shake and thunder as the giant dinosaurs continued their slow lumbering march through the forest. One of the dinosaurs turned and looked at them as if recognizing who they were. It turned its head up and roared, as if greeting them.

"Wow!" the kids yelled.

Hearing the sound of a twig breaking, Thomas turned around and noticed something staring at them through the bushes.

"Uh, Summer," Thomas whispered in a scared voice. "I think there's a lion behind you."

"Ahhhh!" The kids screamed as they ran.

"Wait a second, kids. He won't hurt you. You see, when God first made the animals, sin and death had not yet entered the world," Wizzy told the group.

"You mean the lion won't hurt us?"

"No, and neither will the tiger behind Olive!" Wizzy teased.

"Ohhh, kitty!" Olive said *startled*.

But her attention quickly moved to something else.

"Look! Qwacky is riding an elephant."

"Qwack-a-doodle-dooooo!" cried out Qwacky as he waved his hat in the air.

The elephant's eyes flew wide open and it took off *bellowing* as it ran towards the safety of the forest. Qwacky was thrown high into the air and landed in a puddle of mud. The kid's roared with laughter as Wizzy and Pepe helped Qwacky out of the mud.

Thomas remembered the verse they had just heard and wondered about all the animals they had just seen.

"Wizzy, what does it mean that God made all the cattle?" he asked.

"Well, most Old Testament scholars would say the word cattle is talking about animals God intended for man's use, like: cows, goats, horses, sheep, and camels," Wizzy answered.

"What about when the Bible talks about creeping things?" Summer asked.

"Well, just look down. What do you see creeping on the ground?"

"Snakes!" Summer screamed in terror. Summer did not like snakes at all.

"Cool, that serpent has legs!" Thomas pointed out.

"Hey look! A ladybug," Olive said as she watched a red ladybug crawl up and down her finger.

"Qwibbit! Qwibbit!" quacked Qwacky as he sat on a lily pad next to a bunch of frogs.

"What does it mean when the Bible talks about beasts of the earth?" Olive asked.

"Well, the lion and tiger fit in that category, and

basically all other large animals, both two-legged and four-legged," Wizzy explained to the kids.

"Wizzy, there seems to be a lot of strange animals I don't recognize," Thomas said.

"That's right Thomas, in the beginning there were many *species* of animals which no longer exist. Soon we will find out why. Let us see what God has for us next."

"You mean there's even more?" asked Eli eagerly.

Wizzy looked at him with a smile and said, "God's next creation is the only creation He made in His image!"

"What could it be?" wondered Eli.

"Then God said, 'Let Us make man in Our image, according to Our likeness; and let them rule over the fish of the sea and over the birds of the sky and over the cattle and over all the earth, and over every creeping thing that creeps on the earth.' God created man in His own image, in the image of God He created him; male and female He created them." **Genesis 1:26,27**

"Look over there!" cried Olive. They all ran to where she stood and looked into a clearing. They could not believe what they were seeing.

"Then the Lord God formed man of dust from the ground, and breathed into his nostrils the breath of life; and man became a living being." **Genesis 2:7**

What looked like a clump of dirt began to slowly take shape and look like a man. Suddenly, the man's chest rose as God breathed into the man's nostrils the first breath of life and his eyes opened to the wonders of creation.

"Is that Adam?" asked Eli in awe.

"It smells like him," Pepe quipped.

Wizzy tapped his wrist controller and suddenly the scene changed. They had moved forward in time. Adam was asleep and what looked like a rib bone was transforming into another person. It was a lovely woman.

"So the LORD God caused a deep sleep to fall upon the man, and he slept; then He took one of his ribs and closed up the flesh at that place. The LORD God fashioned into a woman the rib which He had taken from the man, and brought her to the man."

Genesis 2:21,22

"This is incredible!" cried Summer. "Is that Eve?"

"They're so beautiful," Olive said in amazement.

"You know, I think this makes them our great, great, great, great..." Thomas started.

"Great, great, great, great, great...." Olive and Summer continued.

"Super-duper-uper great grandparents," Eli finished.

There was an explosion of laughter among the children.

"You know, that's the first time God said, 'Let Us make.' Before, He said, 'Let there be.' Is there a reason for that, Wizzy?" Summer asked.

"Why yes, Summer. It means God has a special and personal **relationship** with man," Wizzy explained. "He does not have the same relationship with animals, plants, rocks, or the rest of creation."

"Why does it say, 'Let *Us*,' and not 'Let *me*?'" Eli asked. "Were there a lot of people who made man?"

"Yes and no," answered Wizzy to the children's confusion. "You see, there is only one God, but there are three persons: God the Father, God the Son, and God the Holy Spirit, and each one is God. God in three persons is the mystery of the **Trinity**!" So in this case, it means that God the Father, God the Son, and God the Spirit created man! Yet there is only ONE God! That is why it says, 'Let Us.'"

"What? That doesn't make any sense!" Qwacky **blurted** out.

"It is a great and **mysterious** truth, which we don't completely understand, but you see it here in the first chapter of the first book of the Bible," Wizzy told them. "There is one God who exists in three persons, in one being; God the Father, God the Son, and God the Holy Spirit!"

"Astounding!" cried out Eli.

"One God in three persons?" Qwacky said. "My processor is overloading." Black smoke started puffing out of Qwacky's head as he turned in circles *warbling* and wheezing.

"Wizzy, what does it mean that God made us in His image?" Olive asked.

"Well, first of all He made us to live forever. He also gave us the ability to reason and think, which is why we understand things like love, friendship, right from wrong, and language. Like Him, we're builders and inventors, kind of like me, as well as being a creative race. Think about all the art, music, and poetry that man has created over the course of history."

"And remember jokes," Qwacky *interrupted*. "Anybody know what ducks eat with their soup?" he paused for *dramatic* effect. "Qwackers!"

"Qwacky!" the kids giggled shaking their heads.

"But seriously Wizzy, why did God make us?" Olive asked.

"He made us to *glorify* Him by *worshiping* Him and enjoying Him forever," Wizzy answered. "In fact, Isaiah 43:7 says,

"Everyone who is called by My name,
And whom I have created for My glory,
Whom I have formed, even whom I have made."

Isaiah 43:7

"God blessed them; and God said to them,
'Be fruitful and multiply, and fill the earth, and
subdue it; and rule over the fish of the sea and over
the birds of the sky and over every living thing that

moves on the earth.' Then God said, 'Behold, I have given you every plant yielding seed that is on the surface of all the earth, and every tree which has fruit yielding seed; it shall be food for you; and to every beast of the earth and to every bird of the sky and to everything that moves on the earth which has life, I *have given* every green plant for food'; and it was so. God saw all that He had made, and behold, it was very good. And there was evening and there was morning, the sixth day."

Genesis 1:28-31

"And there it is my friends, said Wizzy, "from beginning to end, from the first to the last, God made everything in times past. From the sun, the moon and stars, to the flowers and trees, in six days, God made everything. He even made you, and He even made me!"

The booming voice rang out once again,

"Thus the heavens and the earth were completed, and all their hosts. By the seventh day God completed His work which He had done, and He rested on the seventh day from all His work which He had done."

Genesis 2:1,2

"Whew, I kind of feel like taking a rest myself," said Summer as she let out a big huge yawn.

Wizzy chuckled and said, "But even though God rested from His work of creation, it does not mean that He completly quit working, because He sustains everything — that is He keeps everything going all the time."

"Wow! that's amazing," the kids responded.

"Yes, and that's just the beginning—how it all started. The entire Bible has been given to us by God himself so that we can learn about God and His ways." Wizzy concluded.

Wizzy pressed a button and everything, the trees, the animals, even Adam and Eve, started to fade away. There was a shimmer of light all around them and suddenly, they were back in the Gizmo Shack. The fencing spoons were sleeping on top of an old dish and the robot ants were huddled around the bathroom sink refilling their cups with water.

"Can we do this again?" the kids asked in eager anticipation.

"Of course," Wizzy laughed.

"I'd like to know more about God," said Eli earnestly.

Wizzy smiled kindly and concluded, "It's just like Psalm 119 says,

'Open my eyes, that I may behold
Wonderful things from Your law.'"
Psalm 119:18

The End

(Actually, it is just the beginning.)

Review Questions

All right, kids, time to put on your thinking caps. Let us see how much you remember.

Question: What did God make on the first day of creation?
Answer: The earth and light.

Question: What did God make on the second day of creation?
Answer: He made the firmament. The sky above.

Question: What did God make on the third day of creation?
Answer: He made the land, the oceans, and the plants.

Question: What did God make on the fourth day of creation?
Answer: The Sun, the moon, the stars, and everything else in space.

Question: What did God make on the fifth day of creation?
Answer: Water creatures and birds of the sky.

Question: What did God make on the sixth day of creation?
Answer: Land animals, and Adam and Eve.

Question: Whose image were we made in?
Answer: If you said God's image, you are correct!

Question: What did God tell man to do?
Answer: To be fruitful and multiply.

Question: Who did God put in charge of the Earth?
Answer: God put people in charge!

Question: Why did God create man?
Answer: God made man to worship Him and to enjoy Him forever.

Now, think of three questions of your own, the harder the better. It's okay if you have to look up the answer.

Vocabulary

accelerator - pedal used to speed up

auspicious - having signs of success, or favorable appearances, well timed

bellowing - shouting, yelling

blurted - to say something impulsively, as if by accident

chortled - a gleeful chuckling or snorting sound

complexity - difficulty, complication

creak - squeak

diversity - mixture, variety

dramatic - theatrical, lots of emotion

drone - buzz, hum

eager - excited, ready to go

fervor - earnest feeling

firmament - space, expanse, seperation, the sky

fumbled - slipped, dropped clumsily

gadget - an ingenious device

gaily - joyfully or merrily

gazing - staring, looking fixedly

gizmo - a gadget, especially a mechanical or electrical device

glorify - worship, exalt, praise, adore, honor

groaned - mournful or loud creaking sound

hiss - to make a sharp sound like that of the letter "s"

hyper-intelligent - very smart

infinitely - not measureable, exceedingly great

interrupted - break into a conversation

knobby - having small hard rounded parts sticking out from the surface.

massive - big, bulky, huge

mysterious - unexplained, puzzle, secret

peered - to look narrowly or searchingly

perched - a temporary place for something to rest

pranced - to dance or move in a lively or spirited manner

proximity - nearness in place, time, order, occurrence, or relation

pterodactyls - an extinct flying reptile pterosaur with membranous wings and a rudimentary tail and beak.

quipped - a clever or witty remark or comment

relationship - a connection, association, or involvement

sigh - to let out one's breath audibly, as from sorrow, weariness, or relief.

skimmed, skimming - pass closely over the surface of something

species - a basic biological classification

startled - scare, catch by surprise, shock

throbbing - to beat rapidly and forcefully, as in an injury

throttled - choked

transforms - changes dramatically

Trinity - three persons in one, the godhead

unmitigated - not diminished in intensity, severity, etc

uproar - noisy or loud disturbance

warbling - singing with changing notes

wistfully - pensive and sad; deep in sad thoughts of something yearned for or lost

worshipping - showing reverence, respect, reverent honor and homage paid to God

Explore the world of Wizzy Gizmo and all of his friends at

WWW.WIZZYGIZMO.COM

Exciting sneak previews of the next book, games, puzzles, flash cards, coloring pages, and other fun activities.

This book is available as an audio drama, and in ebook and audio-book format.

NEXT IN THIS SERIES

Book Two

In His Image